NETWORKING

Venture outside your close circle
and connect with other professionals

Written by Elise Evrard

Translated by Jessica Foster

NETWORKING

NETWORKING

- **Issue:** how can I make the most of my contacts to expand my network and reach my professional objectives?
- **Uses:** in many professional situations, a large and diverse network is an irreplaceable asset to improve your visibility, get information or advice, develop new ideas, etc.
- **Professional context:** Job hunting, canvassing for clients, event organisation, career progression, etc.
- **FAQs:**
  - Isn't working on my network akin to 'using' the people around me?
  - Where and when should I network?
  - What if I'm shy?
  - How can I create a network of contacts if I have no time?
  - How can I interest others if there is not a lot to talk about?
  - I never know how to approach people, what should I do?

    "The richest people in the world build networks; everyone else is trained to look for work."
    Robert T. Kiyosaki

We have all heard stories of friends who have found work through friends of friends: Pete who met his future employer through his uncle's gardener; Sophie who talked about her art project to her Pilates instructor, who talked about it to his wife, who happened to know a colleague's husband who could help her; or John who met his best client at a conference. Perhaps you said to yourself, "How lucky!"

But what if these meetings were nothing to do with luck?

Pete, Sophie and John simply knew what to do in order to make the most of a contact with a professional aim. We all have contacts: our family, our friends, our former colleagues, our team mates, our neighbours, etc. And learning how to work with your network of contacts is what we call 'networking'. This method consists of creating or strengthening a network of contacts in the long term for exchanges of knowledge, services or passions among professionals.

In the digital age, human relationships are often neglected. The values of sharing, exchange and mutual aid are sometimes considered ridiculous in the world of work. However, they can bring you more than money or a degree can. Are you looking for your dream job? Do you want to get promoted within your company? Are you looking for new associates or customers? Do you want to meet other people who work in your sector to exchange your knowledge? Learn the art of networking and become a networker in the making!

LEARNING TO NETWORK: THE BASICS

WHAT IS NETWORKING?

Networking means using your network of contacts in the context of professional exchanges. Being a good networker is, more than anything, a state of mind: it means being open to meeting people and collaborating with them. You can then take advantage of this network of contacts to reach your professional objectives.

Did you know that most job announcements are circulated around networks before being publicised? Today, if we want to stand out, networking is an incomparable ally and a powerful professional tool that will lead you to success, as long as you use it wisely.

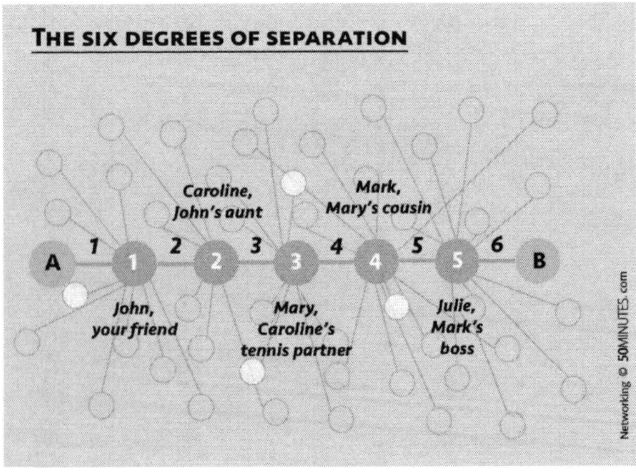

The rise of social networks is not due to Facebook or LinkedIn. This type of network has actually been analysed since 1929, when Frigyes Karinthy, a Hungarian writer, introduced his theory of the six degrees of separation. Have you already been surprised at how small the world is upon realising that the guy you met on the other side of the earth knew one of your friends or family members? Frigyes Karinthy's theory hinges on this idea, and states that anyone, anywhere on the planet can be in contact with any other person via five individuals, one of whom is a direct personal contact.

The world is small: fact. A good network should therefore allow you to reach the person you wish to meet, whoever they are. And there are now tools that can do this work for you: Viadeo and LinkedIn can show you, in just a few clicks, the intermediary contacts that will lead you to the person you wish to reach.

> "I found my first job thanks to networking. I had just finished university and was getting graphic designer jobs on the side from people I knew. The boyfriend of a friend I was at university with was working for a technology start-up who were looking for a profile just like mine. He therefore suggested it to me and I went to their offices. While I was there, I ran into another acquaintance, also an alumna of my university. Out of around twenty people who were employed by the company, I already knew two who could recommend me to their boss after my interview. Proof if proof were needed: the next morning at 9am, I had the job."
> Thomas, product designer and graphic designer.

> "Networking forms the basis of all progression towards a
> senior role. That, among other things, was what helped me
> to move from a junior role to the role of vice-president in 10
> years. [...] I was able to meet the most senior directors of the
> company on a global level, in person. That was only possible
> through networking."
>
> Mark, vice president of a financial institution.

HOW DO I CREATE A NETWORK?

Meeting IRL (In Real Life)

Despite the digital age in which we are living, nothing beats real meetings for creating and expanding your network of contacts. And there is no shortage of opportunities to meet interesting people: talks, conferences, debates, shows, training workshops, professional or social events, work parties, office-sharing spaces, exhibitions, competitions, school and university reunions, etc. Target your events based on your profile, your main interests and, above all, your plan.

During these events, it is important to be natural, but that in no way means that you shouldn't prepare. That is what Laure-Anne, Social Editor and Food Expert, explains to us: "I allow for spontaneity, but of course I make sure I outline, in a few words, what my work consists of, and give a rough idea of my portfolio of clients and so forth."

- Before the event:
  - Do some research on the people who will be there (via LinkedIn for example). You can even contact them to let them know that you would be delighted to meet them.

- Share the event on social networks so that people know you will be there.
- On Twitter, follow the event's hashtag; keep doing this during and after the event.
- Prepare a short, 30-second presentation on yourself – this is what is known as the "Elevator Pitch".
- Prepare your business cards.

THE ELEVATOR PITCH

Imagine that you are in a lift with the CEO of the business you have always dreamed of working for. You have to introduce yourself efficiently in under 30 seconds: this is what is known as an "Elevator Pitch".

During a networking event, you will have to introduce yourself countless times and in a very short amount of time. It will therefore be essential to stir your listener's curiosity, so that he or she only wants one thing: your business card. Your pitch must be short, interesting and captivating, while indicating who you are, what you are offering, what your unique selling point (USP) is and how this can benefit the other person. In summary:

- be clear and concise;
- be different and original;
- identify your USP;
- do not speak too fast and leave pauses at opportune moments;
- only give the essential information;
- prepare and practice your pitch in advance so that

- During the event:
  - Arrive early. That way you can talk to the organisers who can certainly introduce you to the other participants who have arrived early.
  - Smile and always be positive.
  - Never criticise your former or current bosses or colleagues behind their backs.
  - Do not give out your business card to everyone, as giving it to everyone is tantamount to giving it to no one. Filter your contacts and only give out your card if someone asks for it.
  - Relax and have fun. Go towards others and others will come towards you.
  - Listen to the other attendees sincerely and attentively – for example, don't look around for your next conversation partner while someone is talking to you.
  - Ask questions and suggest potential collaboration at the right time.
  - Let the other guests have the chance to meet other people. Try not to talk for longer than five minutes, let the conversation end naturally, thank your listener and do not forget to take his business card.
- After the event:
  - React to the event on social networks. You could potentially forge links with people who share your opinions.
  - Keep your commitments. If you have spoken to another attendee about an article, send it to him or her by

email without delay.
- ○ So that you aren't forgotten, send a quick message to everyone you met, connect with them on LinkedIn and potentially suggest that you continue your conversation over a drink.
- ○ If you have arranged a meeting during the event, confirm it.

Virtual meetings

Networking is sharing, and is there a better tool than the internet for that? The web has dozens of social networking sites for that, all incredibly useful for filling your address book. Whatever your profile or project, there is a social network for you.

- LinkedIn: the ultimate professional social network! It is the ideal place to nurture professional relationships with your former colleagues, your university peers or your future bosses. If you want to stand out from the millions of other users, fill out your profile completely: put up a photo, describe your qualifications and experience and be precise in your descriptions. Then add people to your network by inviting them personally or by asking LinkedIn to suggest contacts.

THINGS TO AVOID

- Do not post a profile photo with your child or group of friends: opt for a professional photo in

which you are the only person.
- Do not send out default invitations: when you invite someone to join your network, delete the default text and write an original, personalised invitation.
- Do not be passive: your new contacts are not going to appear out of thin air, join groups that are related to your interests and be active.
- Do not play down your experience: failing to mention your summer jobs, former jobs and volunteer work is a mistake. Recruiters find this more important than you might realise.

- Viadeo: the first European professional social network, more concentrated on Europe and the emerging markets. Nothing is stopping you from signing up to both LinkedIn and Viadeo. On the contrary: this will increase your chances of filling up your address book.
- Twitter: you cannot imagine what communication in just 140 characters can do for your career! Follow people who interest you and stand out through your originality, just like Thomas, product designer and graphic designer:

> "On Twitter, I try to give myself legitimacy as a designer and web operator. This takes time (months, even years) and you need to share quality content and find your communication style. But this does pay off in the end: people who work in the same sector eventually follow me or have exchanges with me on subjects that we find interesting. The exchanges are therefore productive and, above all, relevant."

- Facebook: the leader of social networks for a general audience. While some people prefer to keep Facebook for their private life, others use this network with professional objectives, like Ben, a web marketer:

  > "My Facebook page is not limited to a closed circle of friends. I open it up to various people, some of whom I do not know yet. Through reflections or humour, I enter into contact with people who I later meet. I share photos and information about my personal life, but nothing too intimate. I show my personality through my posts."

  In addition, nothing is stopping you from keeping your account private and creating a professional Facebook page.
- Google Plus: the largest social network in the world after Facebook. You can share content, create circles of contacts within your networks and create a business page from your personal account in order to connect to other users.
- Pinterest: this is a platform that allows you to create boards by 'pinning' things that interest you. Do you make dresses or design fabulous cupcakes? This site, whose audience is primarily female, is perfect for you! Pin your best creations and connect with people who share your interests.
- Instagram: this is the most popular photo-sharing app in the world. Create an attractive account with a well-defined theme, follow influential people in your sector and, above all, inspire others with your own photos!
- Flickr: a photo and video sharing site which is especially dedicated to image professionals. Are you a photo-

grapher, painter, artist, designer or graphic designer? Be visible on Flickr and connect with other photography enthusiasts. And do not forget to use hashtags so that your photos are well-referenced on the site.
- Myspace: this networking website is indispensable if you are a musician. Your personalised web page will allow you to present your musical compositions to the general public. On a related note, did you know that some artists' Myspace pages are visited more than their official sites? Launch yourself and create your own musical universe if you want to stand out from others.

MAINTAINING YOUR NETWORK: WHY AND HOW?

What do you think would happen if you only reached out to your contacts when you needed their help? You have surely already received a self-interested phone call from someone you haven't heard from in years. It is frustrating and does not necessarily make you want to help them. This is why it is important to keep up with your network through regular, selfless contact. So how should you do this?

- Follow your contacts' activity and congratulate them on their professional successes, or when they get a new job, for example.
- Call to say hello from time to time. There is nothing better than this to pleasantly surprise your contacts and strengthen your network.
- Make your annual newsletter or season's greetings original.

- Have you come across an article that might interest one of your contacts? Send it to them!
- Regularly organise real meetings (meals, reunions, etc.).
- Make sure to 'like' or comment on your contacts' Facebook statuses from time to time.
- Remember important dates. Did your colleague have a crucial presentation today? Ask them how it went. They will be touched that you remembered.
- Do someone a favour whenever you can.

THE NETWORKER: AN OPPORTUNIST?

Using your network of contacts to achieve your ends might seem opportunistic. Bear in mind, however, that networking works from the principle of mutual help. This is not about taking everything you can and giving nothing in return. As Damien Colmant, a business coach, explains to us, "The three ingredients for a good networking attitude are: giving, asking and thanking. Just like a cooking recipe, forgetting one of the ingredients will probably be fatal."

Giving, asking, thanking

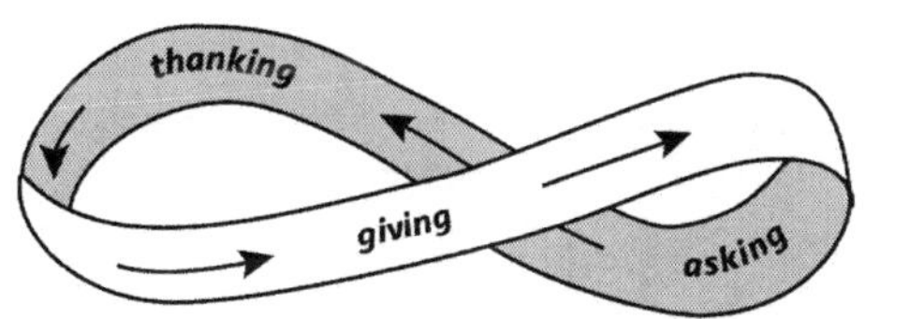

- Give: in networking, the most active people receive the most. Don't stand around figuring out if it will pay off! Offer your help as soon as the opportunity presents itself. First and foremost, you will have the satisfaction of having been useful and you will gain even more in return.

> "I worked for Groupon Belgium for 18 months. There I met Annalies, a Dutch-speaking colleague who I soon began working with on a daily basis. I was then employed by Havas Media. When we had to find a new Dutch-speaking talent, I introduced Annelies to the team manager and she was offered a job. I myself had also got the job at Havas Media through someone I had studied with."
> Laure-Anne, Social Editor and Food Expert.

- Ask: don't rely on others guessing what you want from them. Express your requests clearly and respectfully to give them the opportunity to help you.
- Thank: a 'thank you' costs nothing, but is worth a great deal. Your contacts risk no longer wanting to help you if you never thank them. Be sincere in your thanks and clearly express what you appreciated.

DID YOU KNOW?

While networking can be a stepping stone to getting your dream job or sending your career to dizzying heights, it does not stop there. Networking can also allow you to:

- get to know more people: contacts will more easily remember who you are if they can put a face

to a name;
- become more personally enriched;
- demonstrate your creative spirit by exposing your own ideas;
- learn more about the professional techniques of your peers;
- be informed about the latest trends in your sector;
- broaden your perspectives;
- obtain new ideas and knowledge;
- gain valuable information before others;
- benefit from the advice of more experienced colleagues;
- introduce people in your network to one another;
- find out the opinions of other people on a future service provider, for example.

TOP TIPS

- Do not simply wait for great opportunities to enrich your network. Be open to daily encounters: at the gym, in a queue or during an evening out with friends. A good "networking attitude", according to Thomas, product designer and graphic designer, means "remaining open and interested to others and what they do. Also, be proactive: if you do not run after people, they will not run after you either."
- When an event is happening, do not be the last person to know about it. To keep up to date with future events, subscribe to newsletters from people or organisations in your sector, follow the blogs and Twitter accounts of influential people, join groups on LinkedIn and Viadeo, 'like' Facebook pages for your town or for certain organisations, etc.
- Are your qualifications and experience more chaotic than traditional? Great! Your uniqueness is your best asset. Emphasise it.

> "I have a slightly hybrid profile in that I studied marketing and advertising and began a career as a digital designer. I always take the opportunity to present both sides of my skillset, and often either one or the other allows me to connect with the person in front of me."
> Thomas, product designer and graphic designer.

- During events, be natural and relaxed, talk to as many people as possible and respect the "five-minute rule". You are there to meet people; so are the others. Be interesting, but do not monopolise your listeners. You can always continue the conversation at a later meeting.

- Tell stories that will make people remember you: this is what is known as storytelling.
- Maintain your network. It is crucial to remind the people in your network that you are there, "and, in particular, to use Twitter as much as possible. Don't think twice before following a company you like, highlighting their good work when they launch a new product, or following people who work in the company itself," reminds Thomas.
- Talk about your plans to those around you, even to people who do not seem capable of helping you. Life sometimes has surprises in store for you!

> "I found my job because a Facebook friend saw I was looking for one. She asked me to send her my CV, gave it to some people she knew in several agencies and, a week later, I had three firm offers."
> Candice, new media business consultant

- Listen! "In fact, the best networkers are often great listeners, as opposed to great talkers." (Myers, 2007: 5).
- Be open-minded and nice to everyone! Networking is not about creating a new circle of friends. You can quite easily create a strong, sincere working relationship with someone who is very different from you.
- Give without counting the costs to yourself, because feeling useful gives you value and you will reap the rewards later on. Helping others also allows you to constantly reaffirm your presence.

> "I offer help when I think it is necessary, without waiting for

someone to ask me for something. And I let the people in my network know that the interest goes both ways."
Mark, vice president of a financial institution.

- Be daring! To make progress, you need to take risks. Get out of your comfort zone and go to meet other people without thinking twice about it. Don't be afraid to be different from other people: your originality is what will make you stand out from the crowd.

FAQS

ISN'T WORKING ON MY NETWORK AKIN TO 'USING' THE PEOPLE AROUND ME?

Networking is only effective if the interest is reciprocal. You may of course feel tempted to take as much as possible without ever giving in return, but the other members of your network will realise what you are doing very quickly and will no longer be motivated to help you. You then risk losing their trust and excluding yourself from this network of contacts that you have constructed.

EXTRA INFORMATION

Be aware that reciprocity does not mean immediate return on your investment. Do favours for others and be available if you want to build strong interpersonal relationships. By being an active member of a network, the other members will automatically think of you when the opportunity to recommend you presents itself. In the same way as a farmer, sow generously and you will reap the rewards of your efforts in due time.

WHERE AND WHEN SHOULD I NETWORK?

Creating and expanding your network can be done anywhere and at any time. Perhaps you do not know it yet, but your neighbour might know an influential person in your sector, or your hairdresser might talk about your artistic project to her father-in-law who happens to be the director of an art gallery. Talk to the people around you and trust the power of word-of-mouth.

As well as these chance relationships, it is also essential to meet people who can directly influence your plan or project. To do this, having clearly defined objectives is essential. Are you a musician trying to get noticed? Go to concerts, busk and share your videos on your YouTube™ channel. Do you make jewellery and want to sell it? Go to a traders' exhibition and join Facebook groups dedicated to fashion. In short, target your events, and you will gain efficiency.

WHAT IF I'M SHY?

Firstly, you should know that shyness is a normal phenomenon. Tell yourself that when you go to an event where you do not know anyone, most of the other people there are in the same situation as you. In fact, it is completely normal to feel a little intimidated when you are confronted with people you do not know. Did you know, for example, that Napoleon and Jacques Brel were both extremely shy? That didn't stop them from achieving great things, however.

Shyness is not a fault, but rather part of your temperament and your charm. Don't let it be an obstacle to your dreams and plans, or let it make you miss opportunities and enriching encounters. Remind yourself that nobody is perfect and follow these tips when you initiate conversation with a person you don't know:

- Listen to the other person and react to what they say

instead of thinking about what you could say next.
- Ask open questions to keep the conversation flowing. Instead of asking, "Did you like the conference?", ask, "What did you think of the conference?".
- Do not panic if there is a pause in the conversation. This is completely natural and does not mean that you are not interesting.
- Make eye contact with the other person and smile.
- Be yourself, your personality will do the rest.
- If you are really nervous, say so! You will feel much better and your listener will be the first person to reassure you and put you at ease.
- Bring a friend – but don't just stick to each other, or you risk meeting no one else.

HOW CAN I CREATE A NETWORK OF CONTACTS IF I HAVE NO TIME?

Remember that networking is a way of life that can be done everywhere, and at any time. A networking activity can very easily be integrated into your schedule. For example, never eat lunch alone. Take advantage of mealtimes to share them with a colleague or someone outside your company. You can also very easily expand your network of contacts on a daily basis: when you are chatting to other parents at the school gate, at a gym class, during a family meal, while you are out with friends, etc. Do not forget that building a network takes time and the results are not immediate.

"In the end, building a network is a slow process. A farmer sows seeds knowing that he will only be able to harvest six

to nine months later. In the meantime, he will have invested time into nurturing his field. Just like the farmer, you know that you will have to wait before your networking efforts yield results. The reason is that you have to respect people's timings, create links, maintain them and accept that you will make mistakes."
Damien Colmant, business coach.

HOW CAN I INTEREST OTHERS IF THERE IS NOT A LOT TO TALK ABOUT?

The art of listening is more important than the art of conversation. A person who listens will more easily find favour with the person they are speaking to than a person who launches into an endless monologue. With this in mind, do not put too much pressure on yourself.

Show interest in the other person and let them speak about their business, clients or passions. Then identify the things you have in common and use them. Have they mentioned their tennis match from the day before and you yourself, as it happens, play tennis? Tell them. No one is asking you to talk about the geopolitical situation in Lebanon or the reproductive process of the Argentine ant.

Meeting someone is not the time to show off your intelligence. Anyway, being intelligent and being interesting are not at all the same thing. Speak enthusiastically about subjects that interest you and your listener will instantly find you interesting. Finally, if your lack of conversation is making you anxious, prepare in advance by getting informed about the topic of the evening, for example, and practising some anecdotes that are guaranteed to interest anyone: "Did you know that this exhibition was set up by Woody Allen?". In any case, tell stories, everyone likes those.

I NEVER KNOW HOW TO APPROACH PEOPLE, WHAT SHOULD I DO?

Even if you are comfortable in the discussion, it is not always easy to approach someone you do not know.

- Start by reminding yourself that most of the attendees have also come alone and just want to talk to you.
- Give others the opportunity to approach you by bringing an original accessory with you: a name badge in the shape of a cake if you like baking, an original T-shirt which will draw in comments from the other guests or earrings that you made yourself.
- Another important factor: wear clothes that showcase you and in which you feel good. You will make a good impression and will be able to approach people more easily if you are comfortable in your clothes rather than wobbling on ten-centimetre high heels.
- In conclusion, make the most of the event and have fun! You will have a good time and make others want to come and talk to you. After all, who wants to talk to the grump sipping from their glass alone in the corner?

OVER TO YOU

It is now time for you to get started. Not tomorrow, but today! Remember that the main quality that will make you a good networker is your motivation. Not sure where to start? Follow these exercises step by step and get stuck into the exciting adventure of networking.

YOUR CONTACTS

Do you feel like you are starting from nothing and it scares you? Forget this idea! Without knowing it, you have already been networking and your network of contacts already exists. Like everyone else, you know an unbelievable amount of people. You only need to look at the number of friends you have on Facebook to be reminded of that. By interacting with these people, you are already reaping the rewards of networking. Take a piece of paper and a pen, and do the following:

- Make a list of 20 people you know and, next to it, the link that connects you, as well as three key words that characterise them. For example: Eric Smith, colleague – accounting, tennis, theatre.
- Write down three favours that your contacts have done for you at one point. For example: last summer, my neighbour lent me his dad's lawnmower to mow my lawn.
- Write down three favours that you have done for your contacts at one point.

For example: when my former colleague Caroline lost her job, I spoke about her to my employer and she now works in my team.

As you can see, your network already has interesting contacts in it and you have already tried out networking. Now, all you need to do is enrich your network and consciously manage it.

YOUR PLAN

You will not be a good networker if you do not have a clearly defined plan. Without one, you risk meeting many people without knowing why, and losing your credibility in the eyes of others. Set out your plan by answering the following questions:

- What are your skills? What are the things you know how to do and like to do?
- What do you want to do? Complete this sentence: in an ideal world, I would love to be...
- What is stopping you?
- What could you implement to achieve your plan?
- Make a list of what is a priority for you (salary, workplace, fulfilment, etc.).

THE 'ELEVATOR PITCH'

Remember the importance of the elevator pitch, especially if you feel uncomfortable introducing yourself to someone who does not know you. The pitch must be short, interesting and captivating, while indicating who you are, what you are offering, what your USP is and how that can benefit the other person.

- Write your pitch in a maximum of ten lines.
- Recite it for three different people (friends, colleagues or family members).
- Rework it, bearing in mind the comments of your listeners.
- Recite it again and again, until you are perfectly comfortable.

STORYTELLING

As stated earlier, telling captivating stories incites the interest and attention of your listeners. Do you perhaps tell yourself that you never have stories to tell? This is untrue. You are simply unprepared.

Try to remember three authentic and exciting stories that have happened to you in your lifetime and train yourself to tell them well. The stories do not necessarily have to have a link to your professional life.

SOCIAL NETWORKS

Identify the most appropriate social networks for your plan and, if you have not done so already, sign up. Do not neglect the creation of your profile and invite people to connect with you. If you have already signed up, have a clean-up. Organise your contacts, complete your profile and publish content.

We want to hear from you!
Leave a comment on your online library
and share your favourite books on social media!

FURTHER READING

BIBLIOGRAPHY

- Colmant, D. (2008) Le networking à la portée de tous ? *Horizons Saint-Michel*. Issue 66, pp. 11-13.
- Fletcher, L. (2007) Career Hub: Insider's Guide to Networking. [Online]. [Accessed 4 November 2016]. Available from: <http://careerhub.typepad.com/careerhub_guide_to_networking.pdf>
- Tactic web (No date) *Le networking : un outil essentiel pour développer son business.* [Online]. [Accessed 7 March 2015]. Available from: <http://tacticweb.fr/27-03-2013/non-classe/le-networkingun-outil-pour-le-business/article2867>
- Michael Page (No date) *Le Networking, ou comment utiliser son réseau.* [Online]. [Accessed 4 November 2016]. Available from: <http://www.michaelpage.fr/advice/carri%C3%A8re/votre-recherche-demploi/le-networking-ou-comment-utiliser-son-r%C3%A9seau>
- Connexion carrière. *Le réseautage.* [Online]. [Accessed 7 March 2015]. Available from: <http://connexioncar-riere.ca/vos-outils/reseautage>
- Misner, I. R. and Donovan, M. R. (2008) *The 29% Solution: 52 Weekly Networking Success Strategies.* Texas: Greenleaf Book Group Press.
- Zack, D. (2010) *Networking for People Who Hate Networking.* San Francisco: Berrett-Koehler Publishers.

ADDITIONAL SOURCES

- Anderson, S. (2015) *The Networking Book: 50 Ways to Develop Strategic Relationships*. London: LID Publishing.
- Lowndes, L. (2014) *How to Talk to Anyone: 92 Little Tricks for Big Success in Relationships*. London: HarperCollins.
- Networking Resources. (No date) *University Career Center: University of Michigan*. [Online]. [Accessed 4 November 2016]. Available from: <https://careercenter.umich.edu/article/networking-resources>

IMPROVE YOUR GENERAL KNOWLEDGE

IN A BLINK OF AN EYE !

www.50minutes.com

www.50minutes.com

Ebook EAN: 9782806279347

Paperback EAN: 9782806291240

Legal Deposit: D/2016/12603/867

Cover: © Primento

Digital conception by Primento, the digital partner of publishers.

Made in the USA
Monee, IL
07 July 2026